THE LEPRECHAUN
LIBRARY

BUTTERFLIES

Linda Sonntag

HUTCHINSON

London Melbourne Sydney Auckland Johannesburg

'To a Butterfly'

Stay near me – do not take thy flight!
A little longer stay in sight!
Much converse do I find in thee,
Historian of my infancy!
Float near me; do not yet depart!
Dead times revive in thee:
Thou bring'st, gay creature as thou art!
A solemn image to my heart,
My father's family!

Oh! pleasant, pleasant were the days,
The time, when in our childish plays,
My sister Emmeline and I
Together chased the butterfly!
A very hunter did I rush
Upon the prey; – with leaps and springs
I followed on from brake to bush;
But she, God love her! feared to brush
The dust from off its wings.

WILLIAM WORDSWORTH

Butterfly Records

The largest butterfly in the world is the giant birdwing, found in the Solomon Islands. The female's wingspan can be over 1 foot (30 cm).

The smallest butterfly in the world is the dwarf blue of South Africa, which has a wingspan of under ½ in (14 mm), though the smallest known of all lepidoptera is a moth with a miniature wingspan of only ¹/₁₀ in (2 mm) and a body of the same length.

The butterfly is not by any means the fastest flying insect, but the speed of migratory species has been measured and is remarkable for such a fragile creature. The painted lady has been observed flying at speeds of 5-9½ mph (8-15 km/h), but probably the fastest known migrating butterfly is the monarch, which can keep up with a car travelling at up to 24 mph (40 km/h). Even slow-flying butterflies have been known to cover distances of up to 99½ miles (160 km) in a single day.

The longest recorded flight ever made by a single insect is just under 3000 km in a period of 130 days.

Colour and Camouflage

The lovely iridescent colours of the butterfly's wings are produced either by normal pigmentation or by a method more ingenious to human minds: light refracting on the scales. This causes the dazzling effect of changing colour as the wings move and our angle of vision is altered.

The butterfly's shape, as well as the patterns and colours it displays, is often used as camouflage. The leaf butterfly has markings on its wings which suggest veins and even leaf decay. It alights with its head down and its tail touching the stem like a stalk, making it very difficult to distinguish from real leaves.

The underside of the brimstone's wing looks like an ivy leaf, and it fixes itself to the plant in winter to hibernate.

The Chinese character moth has the dubious distinction of looking like a bird dropping, while the peppered moth has formed two different varieties which merge perfectly with its background. The black peppered moth disappears against the brickwork of sooty townscapes while its country cousin, the white peppered moth, prefers the unpolluted atmosphere of rural districts.

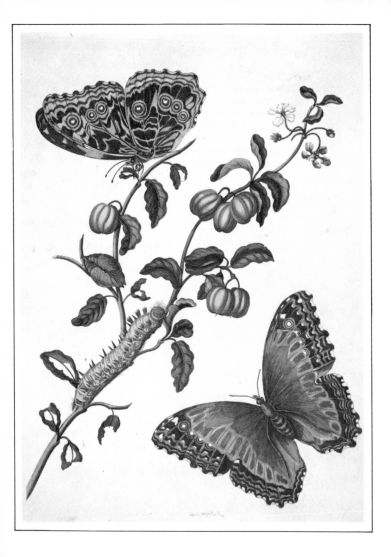

Butterfly Superstitions

All over the world, different peoples harbour different superstitions relating to butterflies. A common belief is that the butterfly represents the soul. The Solomon Islanders claim that when a man dies the door of his house is flung open and his soul takes flight heavenwards in the form of a gorgeous butterfly. Of all the creatures on earth, he has chosen this form for his reincarnation.

In Brunswick, Germany, they say that if the first butterfly of the season that you see is white, there will be a death; if it is yellow, there will be a birth; and if multicoloured, a marriage is imminent.

In Essex, one of England's eastern counties, it is thought that if you catch the first white butterfly you see and bite off its head before letting it go again, you will have good luck for a year. Another way of ensuring good fortune is to make the butterfly fly through the sleeve of your coat – or, for success in hunting, to put a butterfly up the barrel of your gun.

Butterfly Moments

Net in hand, I would dash across the deserted Franciscan churchyard or through the new cemetery; I knew the hidden nooks and crannies in the rotting willow in which butterflies could be found, and where, as the sap trickled down from its cracked bark, I would find the Red Admiral butterfly. The graves were smothered in flowers, dog roses, double roses and, buried in them, the golden heads of Cetonia aurata. I chased like a young savage past the new cemetery across a huge field of flowering clover. There I could easily catch – even without the net – the Urticae butterfly, the Cardui, the Polychroros, C Album, the Io and also the Atlanta and Antiope. In the distance a Papillio Padalirius would occasionally fly up. It was a charming sight, this great flowering field heavy with the scent of honey, full of animation, busy with buzzing flies, moths, bumble bees and bees.

FRANTIŠEK HRUBŮ

Flights of Fancy

The butterfly,
Even when pursued,
Never appears in a hurry.

GARAKU: HAIKU

The toad beneath the harrow knows
Exactly where each tooth-point goes;
The butterfly upon the road
Preaches contentment to that toad.

RUDYARD KIPLING

There never was a king like Solomon
Not since the world began
Yet Solomon talked to a butterfly
As a man would talk to a man.

RUDYARD KIPLING

He said 'I look for butterflies
That sleep among the wheat:
I make them into mutton-pies,
And sell them in the street.'

LEWIS CARROLL

Free Spirits

Walt Whitman, the great American poet, believed passion-
ately in liberty, equality and fraternity. A recluse who spent
much of his time observing nature, perhaps it was his love of
freedom which attracted him particularly to butterflies.

Over all flutter myriads of light-yellow butterflies,
mostly skimming along the surface, dipping and oscil-
lating, giving a curious animation to the scene. The
beautiful spiritual insects! Straw color'd Psyches! Occasionally one of them leaves his mates, and mounts,
perhaps spirally, perhaps in a straight line in the air,
fluttering up, up, till literally out of sight. In the lane as
I came along just now I noticed one spot, ten feet
square or so, where more than a hundred had collected,
holding a revel, a gyration-dance, or butterfly good-
time, winding and circling, down and across, but
always keeping within the limits.

SPECIMEN DAYS

The Butterfly that Stamped

In a beautiful golden palace lived a rich and powerful king called Suleiman-bin-Daoud. He was a kind man but unhappy because his 999 wives were always quarrelling. Sitting in his palace gardens one day, he espied a pair of butterflies arguing as they fluttered above him in a camphor-tree.

'All I have to do is stamp my foot and Suleiman's palace will disappear,' the male butterfly was boasting to his wife. This bold claim made Suleiman laugh. Beckoning to the butterfly, he asked, 'Why did you say that?' The terrified butterfly, recognizing the king, admitted, 'I have to keep her quiet somehow or I get no peace.'

The king laughed even more and told the butterfly to go back to his wife. She immediately wanted to know what the king had said. The reply was: 'Oh, he asked me not to stamp my foot as palaces are very expensive and he didn't want to lose this one.'

The butterfly's impudence made Suleiman roar with laughter. Meanwhile his favourite wife, Balkis, had overheard the conversation. Anxious to see her husband happy, Balkis beckoned to the lady butterfly and asked her to tell her husband to stamp his foot to see what would happen. The butterfly, fearing that his bluff would be called, asked Suleiman what he should do. Amidst tears of laughter the king rubbed his magic ring and four genies appeared. Suleiman instructed them to make the palace disappear when the butterfly stamped his foot. So the butterfly stamped and the palace disappeared. The lady butterfly was terrified and promised never to nag her husband again. Their antics had made the king very happy, which made Balkis very happy too – and, what is more, his wives were so contrite that they stopped quarrelling.

Winged Night

Dark, black, giant butterflies
kill the radiance of the sun.
The horizon, a sealed book
of magic, rests silent.
Up from the vapours of forlorn depths
rises a scent that murders recollection!
Dark, black, giant butterflies
kill the radiance of the sun.
And earthwards from the sky
the monsters invisible,
with heavy pinions, sink
down upon the hearts of men . . .
dark, black, giant butterflies.

ALBERT GIRAUD: PIERROT LUNAIRE

Butterflies and Fairyland

Fair child of Sun and Summer! we behold
With eager eyes thy wings bedropp'd with gold;
The purple shots that o'er thy mantle spread,
The sapphire's lively blue, the ruby's red,
Ten thousand various blended tints surprise,
Beyond the rainbow's hues of peacock's eyes . . .
For thee the rose her balmy buds renews,
And silver lilies fill their cup with dews;
Flora for thee the laughing fields perfumes,
For thee Pomona sheds her choicest blooms . . .

JOSEPH WARTON: 'VERSES ON A BUTTERFLY'

Beautiful, flighty, frivolous, it is no wonder that butterflies are so widely associated with fairyland. The embodiment of both mischief and carefree romance, these decorative creatures have escaped the drudgery of ordinary life to dance in the sun and sip nectar from flowers from dawn till dusk. As portrayed by artists, fairies themselves often closely resemble butterflies, with large, fragile wings and delicate antennae sprouting from otherwise human heads. Certainly they endorse the general impression of fairyland given by poets and artists alike as a place of boundless sweetness and light. Indeed, in many countries butterflies are not merely associated with magic and witchcraft but considered actually to *be* fairies: the Germans and the Japanese claim that their fairy tricks include stealing butter and the cream from the top of the milk.

Butterfly Customs

In Sicily there is a butterfly known as 'the little pig of St Anthony'. It has black wings with red spots on them and is called the little bird of good news. If it flies into your house it will bring you good luck, as long as you greet it with this song:

> In your mouth milk and honey;
> In my house health and wealth.

If a girl wants a new dress, she should catch a butterfly of the desired colour and crush it between her teeth while mumbling a magic formula.

The Serbians believe that the butterfly is the soul of a witch. If you find a sleeping witch, you should turn her body face downwards, then the soul will not be able to re-enter it, and the witch will die.

On St Peter's day in Serbia and Westphalia the children have the special duty of chasing butterflies out of the house. They go about banging on the walls with hammers and chanting special rhymes and incantations until all the butterflies have flown away.

To the Hopi Indians the butterfly is sacred. They set aside one day each year for a ritual butterfly dance to ensure a good harvest. It is performed from dawn to dusk in the village square by the young men and girls while the older villagers look on.

The Gilded Insect

This butterfly necklace in gold and coloured stones was designed and made by René Lalique in the 1890s. Representational themes, especially those of beautiful creatures of the natural world, are the very essence of *art nouveau* design; the fragile appearance of this butterfly is a tribute to the delicacy of the brilliant goldwork and stone-setting of its creator.

Upon the slim, six-legged body of the insect, nature, like a madly inspired couturière, has tried thousands of fabulous colours and cuts and patterns. Man with all his looms and dyes cannot create anything half so exquisite as a butterfly's wing.

The beauty of a butterfly's wing, the beauty of all things, is not a slave to purpose, a drudge sold to futurity. It is excrescence, superabundance, random ebullience, and sheer waste to be enjoyed in its own high rights.

DONALD CULROSS PEATTIE

The Great Lepidopterists

The nineteenth century was the lepidopterists' heyday. Collecting butterflies was a popular hobby amongst the educated middle class, such as doctors and clergymen, who had time on their hands, the inclination to combine leisure with learning and the money to indulge in such pursuits. Some very famous collections, unsurpassed in modern times, were built up in this way. Enthusiasts such as H. W. Bates travelled far and wide and became expert observers as well as collectors. Bates was the first to notice a special type of mimicry in butterflies, subsequently christened 'Batesian mimicry'.

His companion on an expedition to the Amazon was another famous naturalist, Alfred Russel Wallace, Darwin's collaborator , and a man who felt deeply the excitement of the pursuit and discovery of a new species. On capturing his first birdwing, a truly gorgeous butterfly, he wrote: 'On taking it out of my net and opening the glorious wings, my heart began to beat violently, the blood rushed to my head and I felt much more like fainting than I have done when in apprehension of immediate death. I had a headache the rest of the day, so great was the excitement produced by what will appear to most people a very inadequate cause.'

Another collector, A. S. Meek, discovered the largest butterfly in the world, also a birdwing. Since these butterflies fly at a great height, a net held in a human hand was useless, and other means had to be found. In Papua, New Guinea natives were sent scrambling up trees with bows and arrows and rewarded for their finds with tins of bacon and tobacco.

Other now outmoded equipment used by the lepidopterist included a huge unwieldy net almost large enough to trap humans in called the 'two-handled bat folder', an instrument called the 'scissors', which looked like a giant pair of scissors attached to a couple of fly-swatters (and must have done more harm than good), an absurd mechanical decoy that no butterfly could possibly have mistaken for the real thing, and even, as a last resort, a shotgun!

Breeding Butterflies at Home

Butterflies and moths breed prolifically in captivity. Eggs can be bought from breeders and hatched out in a clear plastic box which should be kept out of direct sunlight to avoid the formation of condensation. When hatched the larvae feed on their eggshells and can then be introduced to the foodplant. Choose only clean dry leaves free from disease, and do not overcrowd the box. Clean the box and renew the food supply daily, laying the new leaves gently on top of the feeding larvae. When the larvae are big enough transfer them to a cylindrical breeding cage which you can make yourself from a wooden frame covered with netting. Feed them at this stage on a potted foodplant, which should be changed every other day. Soon they will begin to pupate.

Pupae can be stored throughout the winter in a plastic box in the fridge and returned to the cage about a month before the butterfly is due to emerge: this stage is quite incredible to watch and the most rewarding part of breeding.

Place your adults' foodplant and flowers in plentiful supply at the top of the cage and with any luck they will breed and the whole cycle will start all over again.

Naming the Butterfly

There are over 140 000 known species of butterfly and moth in the world today. Their botanical name is *Lepidoptera* and was coined by the Swedish naturalist Linnaeus from two Greek words meaning 'scale' and 'wing'. The Greeks themselves called the butterfly *psyche*, which means 'soul'. The English name comes from one of two sources: the Anglo-Saxon *butterfloege*, which indicated the yellow colour of the common male brimstone butterfly, or the Old Dutch *boterschijte* (literally 'butter-shit'), which referred to the colour of the cabbage white's droppings.

In other languages the butterfly's name means 'licker of cream', 'milk thief', 'little flag' and, less poetically, 'cabbage shitter'. The Russian *babochka* means 'little soul', and the Spanish *mariposa* 'an effeminate creature which alights'.

Another endearing name has been given to the moth family: Geometridae, which means 'earth-measurers'. They are so called because their caterpillars move with a looping action due to the arrangement of their legs: they have hind- and fore-legs but none in the middle of their bodies. This quaint action also gives them the American name 'inchworm'.

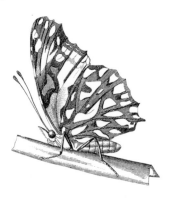

A Noble Insect

Lady Glanville, a seventeenth-century butterfly-fancier, gave her name to the Glanville fritillary, though her hobby earned her only the derision of her family.

'This fly took its name from the ingenious Lady Glanville,' reports one source, 'whose memory had nearly suffered for her curiosity. Some relations that were disappointed by her Will, attempted to set it aside by acts of lunacy, for they suggested that none but those who were deprived of their senses would go in pursuit of Butterflies.'

Though this story is almost certainly apocryphal, it is typical of an age in which butterfly enthusiasts were widely regarded as upper-class eccentrics. The Glanville fritillary itself is found throughout much of Europe, as far north as Scandinavia. In the UK it is found in the Channel Islands and on the Isle of Wight.

Fig. 5.

Fig. 3.

Fig. 4.

Fig. 2.

Fig. 1.

Migration

Butterfly migration is difficult to study scientifically because of the near-impossibility of marking individual specimens with tags, in the way that birds are marked. Miniature tags can be attached to the wing tips but are often lost, causing damage to the butterfly. Mortality is high on long trips and a damaged butterfly is unlikely to survive. An additional problem is that the return trip is rarely made by the same individual because of the butterfly's relatively short lifespan.

One migrating species which has been extensively observed is the spectacular monarch or milkweed butterfly which has its summer home in North America. This amazing creature starts to move south in July, flying by day and feeding en route. Individuals have been known to travel up to 81 miles (130 km) in a single day. At night in poor weather the butterflies roost in trees, but by day they persist even in adverse conditions and are capable of directing their own flight even in the face of 9 mph (15 km/h) headwinds.

The monarch has flown as far as Australia, where it has now established a thriving colony. It also flies across the Atlantic to Great Britain, resting on the sea overnight or taking refuge on ocean-going liners. Canadian monarchs migrate every year to Florida and Mexico, where they have become a popular tourist attraction. The Sierra Madre even boasts a 'Butterfly Mountain', a spot 9000 feet (2700 m) above sea level where the butterflies flock in dense clouds which darken the sky. Here they gather in millions, covering the ground in a gorgeous palpitating tapestry and festooning the trees until they are hidden from sight.

Mimicry

Some butterflies mimic other species to frighten off their predators. Unlike their camouflaged cousins, they are startlingly visible with gaudy colours and bold markings designed to act as a threat and a warning.

One species well worth mimicking is the monarch butterfly, which has strong black markings on brick red and yellow wings: colours that flagrantly advertise that their wearer is inedible, even poisonous. Other perfectly innocuous butterflies fly under these same colours, affording themselves a protection that is entirely bogus.

Some moths mimic wasps and bees, adopting elongated or bumbling body-shapes and yellow and black stripes to indicate danger – where of course there is none.

The enormous Attacus moth has markings on its wing tips which resemble the head of a snake, and the owl butterfly (opposite) uses its striking 'eye' markings to scare off attackers by flicking its wings open and closed in its enemy's face. If a bird does attack it, it will go for the 'eyes'. Thus the butterfly may end up with tattered wings, but a body that is still completely intact.

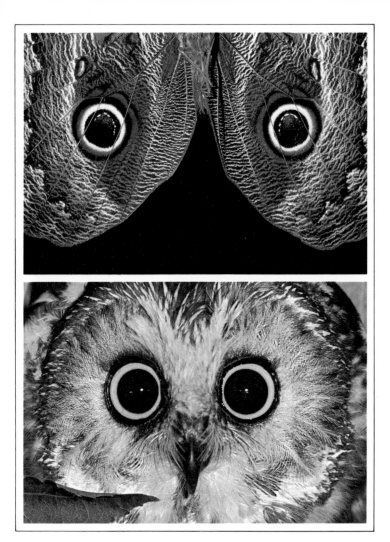

Summer's End

The leaves fall early this autumn, in wind.
The paired butterflies are already yellow with August
Over the grass in the West garden;
They hurt me. I grow older.
If you are coming down through the narrows of the river
   Kiang,
Please let me know beforehand,
And I will come out and meet you
     As far as Cho-fu-sa.

EZRA POUND

Butterflies Aloft

When kite-flying was first invented, in China in the 4th century BC, its purpose was wholly practical. The kites were huge, made of silk and bamboo, and were used for launching men into the sky – condemned prisoners or drunken sailors, very often. One purpose of this was to foretell good or bad fortune, according to an account by Marco Polo, but man-lifting kites were also used for forecasting the weather and as military observation posts. Such kites were not objects of great beauty, and their shape was usually an ordinary rectangle, but during the tenth century the Chinese began flying kites for fun once a year, on the ninth day of the ninth month – the 'Festival of the Ascension' – and the eventual result of this, in the eighteenth and nineteenth centuries, was that the kites themselves became far more intricate. They have been made in the shapes of birds, dragons, fish, dragonflies, human figures, legendary or imaginary creatures and purely abstract conceptions. But for sheer beauty of form and colour, it is not surprising that the butterfly kite has long been a favourite. As you hold the line in your hand, you feel the wind tug the kite away and it breaks free like a living creature, soaring high into the sky and away from human cares.

> Shimmer of butterfly wings – you carry
> Aloft as a cargo of treasures rare,
> The glittering, chilly dew of the morning,
> From the blush of the dawn to the sun's last flare.

FRANTIŠEK HRUBÚ

The Butterfly and the Flame

A beautiful butterfly was flitting through the twilight one evening when he noticed the flame of a candle dancing in an open window. Fascinated by its flickering light, he flew towards it. He flew away, flew back, then made for the flame and skimmed over it.

A moment later he lay stunned beneath the light, the points of his wings singed and smouldering.

But still the flame tempted him and he fluttered lamely back into its golden halo. This time its fierce heat consumed him and he fell, burned, into the oil that fed the flame.

'Accursed light,' murmured the dying butterfly. 'I thought I should find happiness in you and instead I have found death.' 'Poor foolish butterfly,' replied the flame. 'I am not the sun. I am only a light. And those who cannot approach me prudently are burned.'

LEONARDO DA VINCI: FABLE

Butterflies in the Garden

There are as many so-called 'butterfly plants' as there are 'bee plants'. Each butterfly has a favourite foodplant on which it lays its eggs. The caterpillars, once hatched, eat the leaves, while the adults sip nectar from the flowers.

To attract butterflies to your garden, the best idea is to plant as many flowers as possible and avoid the use of insecticides and weedkillers. Amongst the best flowers to choose are those known for their sweet fragrance, such as lavender, aubrietia, sweet william, mignonette, valerian, and especially the mauve-tasselled buddleia, which is often known as the butterfly bush. Other plants that butterflies particularly like include kentranthus or 'Pretty Betsy', sedum, Michaelmas daisy, scabious, lilac, honesty, cornflower, clover, hyssop, forget-me-not, thyme and muscari bluebell. Lobelia is said to hold particular attractions for tortoiseshells.

Butterflies are also attracted to rotten fruit, but if there are no fruit trees around a mixture of apple pulp and stale beer sweetened with brown sugar and smeared on a bird table or fence post, preferably out of reach of cats, will provide a tempting feast.

Papillon

It is not only poets, artists and writers that have been fascinated by butterflies. In the nineteenth century composers such as Grieg, Schumann and Puccini took inspiration from aspects of the butterfly – its flight, its form, its fleeting existence – and the great ballerina Marie Taglioni devised a ballet, *Papillon*, about a young girl who is turned into a butterfly by an evil fairy.

Taglioni came out of retirement to choreograph the ballet for a young protégée, Emma Livry, in whose dancing she saw a reflection of herself as she had been at the start of her career. First performed at the Paris Opéra in November 1860, the ballet was an immediate success, and brought Livry tremendous personal acclaim. Critics praised her light ethereal style and dazzling virtuosity, and audiences were touched by her portrayal of the fragile butterfly. Livry's career as a leading dancer seemed set fair. She danced the rôle at every performance – forty-two in all – for two years. Then disaster struck. In the ballet's finale, the butterfly-girl's wings are burned away as a cupid holds a flaming torch too near her, and this releases her from the spell; during a stage rehearsal, by a strange irony, the skirt of Livry's costume was set alight by the naked flames of one of the winglights, which in those days were run on gas. Horribly burnt, she suffered months of agony before her strength finally deserted her in the summer of 1863.

After this event, the ballet was retired from the repertory and has languished in oblivion for over a century. Now, however, it has been revived and rechoreographed for the Houston Ballet (Texas) by Ronald Hynd to the same Offenbach score used by Taglioni. In this version the closing scenes show the butterfly and her lover burning to death, only to be reunited in eternal love surrounded by their winged companions.

The Killing Bottle

I am one in a row of specimens. It's when I try to flutter out of line that he hates me. I'm meant to be dead, pinned, always the same, always beautiful. He knows that part of my beauty is being alive, but it's the dead me he wants. He wants me living-but-dead. I felt it strongly today. That my being alive and changing and having a separate mind and having moods and all that was becoming a nuisance.

He is solid; immovable, iron-willed. He showed me one day what he called his killing bottle. I'm imprisoned in it. Fluttering against the glass. Because I can see through it I still think I can escape. I have hope. But it's all an illusion.

A thick round wall of glass.

JOHN FOWLES: THE COLLECTOR

The Butterfly Philosopher

Chuang Chou was the most original Taoist philosopher. He was called the Butterfly Philosopher not, as some people believe, because his mind flitted from one delightful idea to another, but because he used to dream he was a butterfly. When he awoke he was not sure whether he was a butterfly dreaming he was a man or a man who had dreamed he was a butterfly. Lao Tzu, his teacher, was reputedly the author and master of the Tao ('Way') itself.

Formerly, I, Chuang Chou, dreamt I was a butterfly, flying about and feeling it was enjoying itself. I did not know that it was Chou. Suddenly I awoke and was myself again, the veritable Chou. I did not know whether it had formerly been Chou dreaming that he was a butterfly, or whether it was now a butterfly dreaming that it was Chou.

Chou asked his teacher Lao Tzu why he felt the sensation of flying in his shoulders on waking. Lao Tzu replied:

Formerly you were a white butterfly which, being partaken of the quintessence of flowers and of the yin and yang, should have been immortalized; but one day you stole some peaches and flowers in Wang Mu Niang-Niang's garden and that is how you came to be reincarnated.

CHUANG TZU, BOOK I

Acknowledgements

The author and publishers are grateful for permission to quote copyright passages from the following books: extract from *The Collector* by John Fowles (Jonathan Cape, 1963); extract (here entitled 'Summer's End') from 'The River Merchant's Wife: A Letter from the *Collected Shorter Poems* by Ezra Pound reprinted by permission of Faber and Faber Ltd 1968 and *Personae* (© 1926 by Ezra Pound) reprinted by permission of New Directions, New York; extract from *Pierrot Lunaire* by Albert Giraud reprinted by permission of Universal Edition (Alfred A. Kalmus Ltd); extracts from Rudyard Kipling's poetry reprinted by permission of A. P. Watt Ltd.

"The Butterfly that Stamped" is an abridgement of one of Rudyard Kipling's *Just-So Stories*.

The author and publishers would also like to thank the following for providing information used in this book: Sadlers Wells Ballet Company, London, for details relating to *Papillon*; and Angus and Robertson for information in Dulcie Gray's *Butterflies on my Mind* (1978) used in the item entitled 'A Noble Insect'.

Illustrations

The author and publishers wish to thank the following for permission to reproduce illustrations and photographs: Peter Bowman, page 17; Jim Channel, page 47; Chester Beatty Library, Dublin, and Elgin Court Cards, pages 7 from *Insectorium Surinamesium* and 55 from *Flowers and Insects* in the style of Sha Ping of Yun Hsi; Bruce Coleman, pages 4, 5, 31, 37 and 39 (above and below); Cooper-Bridgeman Library, pages 15, 19 (*Portrait of Valentine* by Sir Roland Penrose), 22–23 (*Midsummer Fairies* by George Naish), 50–51 and jacket paintings by Tamas Galambos; Peter Cope, page 3; Russell Coulson, pages 9 and 43; Mary Evans Picture Library, pages 29, 52 and 53; Felix Gluck Press Archive, page 35 print by Jan Christiaan Sepp; Michael Holford, page 41; Steve Kirk, pages 12 and 13; Mansell Collection, pages 32 and 33; David O'Connor, page 45; Portal Gallery, page 11 (*Joseph Grimaldi Butterfly Hunting* by Patricia Neville); Nicholas Price, page 25; Sadlers Wells Theatre, Royal Ballet production of *Papillon*, with Margaret Barbieri in title rôle, page 49; Victoria and Albert Museum, Crown Copyright, page 27.

Hutchinson & Co. (Publishers) Ltd
An imprint of the Hutchinson Publishing Group
3 Fitzroy Square, London W1P 6JD

Hutchinson Group (Australia) Pty Ltd
30–32 Cremorne Street, Richmond South, Victoria 3121
PO Box 151, Broadway, New South Wales 2007

Hutchinson Group (NZ) Ltd
32–34 View Road, PO Box 40-086, Glenfield, Auckland 10

Hutchinson Group (SA) Pty Ltd
PO Box 337, Bergvlei 2012, South Africa

First published 1980

Designed and produced for Hutchinson & Co. by

BELLEW&HIGTON

Bellew & Higton Publishers Ltd
19–21 Conway Street London W1P 6JD
Copyright © Bellew & Higton Publishers Ltd 1980
ISBN 0 09 143200 6

Printed and bound in Spain

by Printer Industria Gráfica S.A.
Provenza, 388/Barcelona, San Vicente dels Horts 1980
Depósito Legal B. 16011 – 1980